River Town

dougie padilla

LUNA BRAVA PRESS
Pepin, Wisconsin

Copyright © 2020 by Douglas Padilla

All rights reserved. This book or any portion thereof may not be reproduced or used in any manner whatsoever without the express written permission of the publisher except for the use of brief quotations in a book review or scholarly journal.

First Printing: 2020

ISBN 978-1-7330911-1-4

LUNA BRAVA PRESS
202 Main Street
Box 146
Pepin, WI 54759

www.dougiepadilla.com

Cover photo: Dougie Padilla

Cover design: Pete Sandvik, Perfect Circle Creative

Publications manager: Karen Wilcox

Biography photo: Xavier Tavera

 Dougie Padilla is a fiscal year 2021 recipient of a Creative Support for Individuals grant from the Minnesota State Arts Board. This activity is made possible by the voters of Minnesota through a grant from the Minnesota State Arts Board, thanks to a legislative appropriation from the arts and cultural heritage fund.

LUNA BRAVA PRESS
Pepin, Wisconsin

for James Hillman.

the pepin quartet:

Pepin Diary

River Town

The Breakwater

Coulee Song

"... we are stars wrapped in skin ..."

- jalāl ad-dīn muhammad balkhī

contents

the one who no longer has feet	9
five short poems about winter	11
pelican	14
the art opening	15
2nd street rhapsody	17
it could happen	18
looking for your haiku	20
no rabbits in the dream	21
a kinda hell	24
a short ode to franky gaard	25
sitting outside the breakwater bar	27
i am limping	29
what exactly?	31
two trees	33
it is important to me to talk to birds	34
president spanky still wants a wall	36
love medicine	39
at all costs	41
already	43
a kinda short poem in praise of sun ra	44
river town	47
the poplar leaves	48
on pondering the state of the democracy	49
it's raining	50
a thousand stars	52
the circus gets serious	55
an ambush of poets	56
on kurt vonnegut's assignment	59
standoff	60

contents

similes	61
3 koans	62
i am living inside louise erdrich's novels now	64
the mysteries	66
i gotta get back on the horse	68
brutal #1	70
brutal #2	72
fields of the lord	74
wild thing	75
the light is too flat	76
taking a bath	79
walk away	80
the days and nights have become fluid	81
guinea pig social hour	84
eddie	86
i am studying blake again	89
this chance	91
twelve twelve seventeen	93
toboggan	94
dougie padilla biography	99

the one who no longer has feet

i am the one who no longer has feet,
the one that flies across the sky
like chagall used to do for bella,
in russia after the revolution,
before their move to paris,
before they discovered
their lust for dust
and day old bread.

i have wings now myself,
but not the kind of wings
you would usually recognize.

my wings are made of powder and darkness,
of azure scents and insect smiles.
they come in three sizes,
medium, large, XL.
they have the exact opposite effect
than what you would imagine.

my wings
pin me to the ground
in a body that wants to dissolve,
that wants the shadow lost
behind the china hutch
after dinner in the fifties,
near winona, near calidonia,
near spring grove.

my wings
grab me by the shoulders
and silently push me into the woods,

push me until i know the owl's
constant motion,
see its faint, escaping outline,
a buried shapelessness,
snow bound
and lost
out beyond the sumac.

my wings
write long, slow letters
to ginsberg,
to dante,
to dickenson,
and, maybe even, to ikkyu,

right there
where he sits on a down log,
beside a cold stream,
ice melting off the green banks,
the trout growing ever more alive,

his breathing
the only sound
for a thousand miles.

five short poems about winter

1.

the sun rose at exactly 7:42 this morning.
it sets at exactly 4:51 this afternoon.
that's nine hours nine minutes of sunshine,

which, of course could be worse.
it could be oslo, norway,
they got seven hours and thirty-seven
minutes of sunlight today.

either way though,
not enough.
we need sunlight
otherwise we turn
into gophers,
burrow further and further
down into the darkness,
the dank, cold darkness,
become republicans,
get cable talk shows,
hoard our ample money,
and moan and bitch
about immigrants
being the reason
we're all cursed
and left for dead.

2.

when i was in grade school
i did my paper route at 32 below -

and that didn't count the wind chill
(at 32 below exposed skin
freezes in just minutes).

these days, we gripe about the cold,
about the taste of our spring water,
the way the internet is too slow
downloading movies,
and how the snowplows
were an hour late plowing out
our second home in the lake country
up north.

personally, i prefer to lament
the way a poem ends,
to complain about how a film is structured,
or to bitch about the way the vikings use
their middle linebackers -
you know, important things.

3.

out over the houses of the village
the sun shines a brilliant silver white,
the snow on the lake
pushed into frequent patches
of darkened opalescent gray,
blown away, blown far and wide,
blown into drift
after drift
after drift.

4.

in this deep cold,
the mountains of snow
plowed into the lot
across the street
sit alone,
sit by themselves
sit quietly still,
sit quietly shadow blue.

5.

today,
i lay back on the couch
talking on the phone
to stewart
at his goat farm
north of the cities,
enjoying the melody
of my snoring dog
beside me.

i am moving slow,
very slow,
hunkered down
and ready
for a long,
long winter,

but also ready to sprint
for the bahamas
if i ever get that
check.

pelican

pelican on the water
out beyond the spring ice
right there exactly
where the sun dissolves
into a stretch of silver light.

such a long, skinny neck!

the art opening

from here i can see the graves,
gray in the starlight.
the moon hasn't risen yet,
doesn't want to rise.
i can hear the stories behind the stories,
the stories behind the stones.
i can see off into the beginnings of real darkness
off around the edges,
back into the trees,
away from the road that leads to town
and our lives there.

++++++++

once an artist loses hope
a certain kind of pain takes over.
you begin to press for success.
not real success,
but the money kind of success,
the kind of success
that makes holes in your gut,
that puts a spare tire around your belly,
that makes you heedless of your kids
and their fifth birthday parties.

+++++++

there is a deadness
to the way the light has grown tonight.
time to pile the downed trees
in the corners away from the arbor vitae,
downhill from where the lilies

are starting to dance their way
to the lake.

i want you to look away and remind me
later why you and your art
were buried in that same hole,
in that same ground,

at the same time.

2nd street rhapsody

walking past rob's place
i stick my nose
into white apple blossoms

and the entire world breathes.

it could happen

i'm trying to figure out
a way that my poetry
can drive trump from office.

i'm thinking just the right verb
in just the right sentence
might do the trick,
like letting the air
out of a balloon,
the balloon squealing
across the presidential dining room
after dinner.

or maybe an adjective that hits him
exactly where it hurts would be best,
hits him right in that little ego of his,
down there below his belt,
whereupon he just sits down and gives up,
rolls his pained, bloated body
into a fetal ball
and exits the game.

or maybe, just maybe,
a descriptive poem
pointing out the details
of just one of his small flaws
might set him off like a bomb
and he goes into a mad rage, just
explodes late one night in the oval office,
blood splatter
across the curtains and floor

and out the doorway.

it could happen.

looking for your haiku

From: douglas padilla <artjones@bitstream.net>
Date: December 21, 2009 11:52:08 AM CST
To: hello@carney.com
Subject: Re: The Carney Group is looking for your haiku.

Subject: Re: The Carney Group is looking for your haiku.

reading email, something from pat.

sparrows on the railing in the snow.

i gotta pee.

no rabbits in the dream

i was up half the night with deborah.
there were no rabbits in the dream.
we were in durango,
our cousins knew each other.
we discussed corn.
i don't usually care about corn.

i cannot drink alcohol either,
not at all.
there is too much work to be done.
i cannot sleep now.
the river carries me downstream,
but the words are mushy
and taste like chicken wings
with thai lime sauce
and 3.2 beer.

+++++++

the body is a light thing,
its functions are subtle.
too much food and drink
and the truck with all the children
gets stuck in a ditch
on the side of the road halfway to town.

too little food and drink
and the sound of birds is all we hear,
the grackles endlessly pounding
against the sweeter singing,
chickadees, warblers, meadowlarks.

plus, once the third eye opens
and the sacred heart has been set free,
it's a razors edge to wander this world:
there is grinding everywhere,
cars, freeways, truck stops,
motorcycles with no mufflers,
shopping centers, grocery stores…

once the mind opens up and leaves the body,
you discover walls clanging away,
fresh with discomfort,
pain that sits in the hands all night long.
it can be a challenge to walk the streets.
it can be a challenge to sing in choirs.

better to stay on the deck
and confirm that the sun is setting,
that the chipmunk under the woodpile
is barking in that small high voice we love.
better to work slowly
in the key of e flat minor like bach did.
better to stay away from contracts and grants
and business discussions,
especially, if such is all in the interests
of those that see without eye-lids
and swim without ever sinking.

no, i say glory instead in the way color dances.
paint the blue that can only be seen
by the song that blue is singing,
the brown that can only be seen
from within the exact thought of brown.
encourage the older ones inside the walls
to come out and sit in front of the garage
on folding chairs at evening time,

sit facing the polish church
that has the rummage sales
twice a year
and pierogis for sale
most friday mornings.

a kinda hell

they say that after the body dies
the soul goes thru a tunnel of light
and arrives at paradise,
a place with the greenest grass
and the most beautiful flowers.
they say you are met by those you love,
those you miss the most,
those that truly love you.

donald trump is met by roy cohn.

yes, that roy cohn,
mr. weasel-of-all-time roy cohn,
trump's close friend and mentor,
hatchet man for mccarthy,
bag man for new york city bosses,
poster child for big city corruption.

don's dad doesn't bother to meet him.
his mother isn't available either.
his grandparents on both sides
aren't interested.

roy cohn is all he's got
on the other side.

that's gotta be a kind of hell.

a short ode to franky gaard

i first heard about you
when i was living beneath my work table
down below all my tools,
near the floor
where i do most of my real work.

the word from the street
was that you were a madman,
a man not given to making choices
based on the obtuse calculations
of middle management hierophants,
a man unlikely to bake his thoughts
on cookie sheets,
in casserole dishes
or near any kind of screen door.

then when i first saw your paintings
i had an epiphany of sorts:
the wilder the color,
the brighter the shape,
the more dopamine
rushed thru my lizard brain,
rushed thru and down into my pants
down to the second and third chakras
where i housed all those lingams,
the ones i usually hid behind the shed,
there beneath the wheelbarrow,
there in the shadows of the pines,
closer to the rushing creek
and further from o god so many
endless mortgages.

you see, it appears
that we art world types
need the sunlight provided,
almost exclusively,
at the tip of a brush,
at the edge of a pen.
we need that light to mount us,
to work us, to drive us,
horses in heat,
percherons in the summer fields
pushing their way thru the potatoes,

all the while,
our beloved bardot
dreaming lazily in the sun
on a beach
near cannes,

my indolent
adolescent
self

never
the same

again.

sitting outside the breakwater bar

sitting outside the "breakwater bar",
sailboats jogging across the lake,
winds from the west by southwest
at around 15-20 mph
(i don't know how many knots that is,
i'm not much of a sailing guy).

cars line up along 1st
and the railroad tracks,
all sedate,
all dedicated to their own gods,
all facing southeast.
maybe their mecca is miami or fort lauderdale.
they don't really seem to have faces,
i don't feel like i can really know them.

and no vultures this evening.
nothing floating by across the skies
longing for death and decay.
maybe they're over at the "third base bar",
seems like some guys go there to die,
or maybe just die for the night.

the hydrangeas weave and bow in the wind,
all white and glowing,
the day lilies brash and orange yellow
are speaking in tongues
(like in the bible).

now that i am older i can usually
hear these things.
i can usually see thru wood and plastic

and gravel and neon,
i can usually spot the spirit animals
on the other side.

this place smells of rabbit gods.
i don't know why.
most likely they want to be
this close to water.

i guess there's no accounting
for the way they race wildly
on their quest
for world domination.

i guess it's a tie between them,
the turkeys that swarm the sides of the road
racing madness stylee somewhere or other
as i head into the coulees
to walk the dog,

and the sundry deer hunters
drenched head to toe
in endless blaze orange,
their hearts and minds
set on ransoming the family fortune
with one fell shot.

i am limping

1.

i am limping.
again.
my feet hurt.
this leg doesn't work quite right
until i get it good and warmed up.
seems i'm coming round
the straight-away to 70,
70 with all its pleasures and pains,
a sandman's dream,
castles made of birdsong
and dripping rain,
very quiet longings
dug into the soil,
left here by the grandmothers,
badger tracks aglow
in the evening sky.

2.

i find the daily battle tiring.
i am growing older now.
robert is 90.
doug von koss is getting there.
bob roberts is gone.
vito is gone.
bill wormley is gone.
so is chuck fred.

but the women don't seem to be dying off yet.
they're sitting out by the barn,
shucking corn and making pizza
for their grandsons.
maybe there is a lesson to that,

maybe the men should turn
and face the women.

what exactly?

1.

i woke up this morning and it was still dark.
in the winter the sun rises way too late
and sets way too early.
plus, the skies are gray most of the time.
well, a lot of the time.

i thought i signed up for a warmer, sunnier life.
that contract musta got lost,
along with the one authorizing fame,
and the one bequeathing me
a rather oversized inheritance.

2.

there are weeds alongside the road.
i can feel them in my mouth,
on the lower left where my teeth reach my gums.
they seem to flourish in the lake rocks there -
weeds and beer cans too,
food wrappers from macdonalds,
the remains of a dinner from kfc.
my mind spotted that mess a few weeks back.
i'm sure i'll clean it up,
soon as i take a nap,
watch the game,
write to my sister,
have a glass of wine on the deck.

3.

ok, now the weeds have spread
out beyond my mouth.
i can see them across the street,
out where the emptied houses
create shadows of what used to be our town,
out where there used to be music
and now there is simply dust,
dust made of decaying sunflower stalks

and small piles
of perfectly round
rabbit turds.

4.

so,
dougie,
what exactly
have you done today
to ease the burdens

of just one soul?

two trees

two trees -

some kind of maple

and some other kind of tree
with a multitude
of lightly floating leaves

stage a very slow sit-in
near my park bench.

gray hazy skies
debate

how hot the day will be.

it is important to me to talk to birds

it is important to me to talk to birds.
it is important to me that those birds listen,
that they take the time to sit there
and have a moment
so our friendship can grow.

it is important to me to sit on the deck
and see the elegant future,
what with all its strands racing off ahead,
out beyond the corn and soybeans,
into the woods and ravines
down towards the chippewa.

it is important to me to have grandchildren,
grandchildren that I can touch,
even as they wander the far worlds,
even as they build shacks
made of apples and lilacs.

it is important for me right now,
this very week,
to take a step or two or twenty,
back from the crazy worlds,
the newspaper worlds,
the internet worlds,
the worlds that climb all over each other
strangling life from the dew
the marigolds sleep on.

may those in power
and those out of power

share the beauty of all things,
of all things layered
and endless.

may the birds speak freely
with each and every one of you,
and with each other.
may you listen and respond
in a language you cannot hold
or even dream of.

and may you soar over lake pepin each fall
as you start your everlasting journey southward
for a warmer winter nearer to the sea -
and the lands we all arise from,
the lands we all return to.

president spanky still wants a wall

1.

president spanky still wants a wall.
let's build it with the military's budget.
while we're at it, let's take the money
from preschool childcare and use it
to keep guantanamo open.
speaking of which, we could fund remodeling
our ww2 era internment camps
by cutting back on monies from our
completely unnecessary national park
wilderness areas.
hell, let's eliminate federal college aid
and build my presidential library now
while i can still remember what i'm doing
sorta.

and, the white house could use a do-over.
i mean it's really kinda an eyesore, not
very *au courant*, not very fashionable.
also, the affordable care act is pretty much useless.
so let's take that money and do this place up right.
i mean foreign leaders stop by here -
is asking for a few gold-plated faucets
really too much?

2.

in nebraska dishes are falling off shelves.
the wind has started to curl back on itself.

plum trees are dropping their lovely fruit
out of solidarity, out of regret.

in alabama even the kkk is alarmed.
the football team has watched the red
bleed out of their uniforms, watched
crimson tide tees all across the state turn
a sodden pink, suddenly drained
of their native blood.

and in arizona the desert is blooming, but only
alone and at night and very near the border,
maga cap wearing garbage truck drivers having
lost control of both toothbrush and tollbooth,
their vacant smiles now merely signposts
to the empty interior.

3.

my chair swivels backwards
until i lay horizontal
and stare at the ceiling.

the ceiling stares back at me.

what are we going to do with this guy?
it's hard to fathom how a man
can have absolutely
no keel.

4.

in a very, very expensive hotel room
in las vegas, nevada,

stormy daniels is wondering
how it all got to this.

i mean spanking a grossly overweight
maybe possibly very rich businessman
with a magazine cover for a face
just to finally get his engine revved up
after an evening of cheeseburgers
and sean hannity:

being a porn star has had its moments,
but this is surely not one of them.

love medicine

(for louise erdrich)

this morning,
sunflowers began to bloom
alongside the propane tank out back.
marigolds popped up in the sidewalk cracks
outside tom and kitty's place.
wasps found their way
to the overfilled trash cans
by the "bear's den".

and this morning,
the tourists will come
for the bands and the beer and sunshine.
and the bees and morning glories
will migrate out into the hills
to grab a bit of peace,
out by bogus creek
just upriver off 35 near deer island,
far from the cappuccino bikers
and their designer harleys.

and lipshaw morrisey,
lipshaw morrisey will sit silent,
a quiet young man
on his grandma's front porch,
full moon alive in his hands,
the legacy of generations in his hands,
the humming bird story in his hands,

he will sit o so still,
even as i read *Love Medicine*

for the third time,
out in the backyard under
the shade of a maple tree,
my bare feet sinking
further and further

into the ground

i will be buried in.

at all costs

walking through terminal 2,
san diego airport,
humans flying by randomly
on their way to fish belongings
from snaking airline tributary
conveyor belts,

i wander by a huge huichol yarn painting
half hidden by plexiglass,
its bright ritual mysteries
written in reds and golds and blacks,
buried in glare from overwhelming
lights and windows.

these are stories of peyote,
of peyote gods,
of the deer people,
the burning sun,
the desert home,
the mountains in jalisco.
these are stories
that have no plastic in their dna,
that are born and grow and decay
and return again through the years.
i can feel their smell from where i stand
on the carpeted marble.

but the glare off the plexi is so fierce
i only begin to see
these glorious stories well
when i step back and to the side
and enter from a difficult angle,

dodging

the modern, american urge
to protect everything
at all costs,

in all ways.

already

gray december day
and the grass
is a very dull green.

no snow yet
and i already
long for spring.

a kinda short poem in praise of sun ra

the path down the nile is long,
4258 miles to be exact.
but it's much longer
(or much shorter)
for those who live
in multiple dimensions,
for those who glide
between planets at will.

(have you noticed
that the word jazz
ends in two z's?
how odd.
not many words
have two z's
at the end.
razzmatazz of course.
pizzazz.
whizz, frizz, buzz, fuzz,
a few others...

and jazz).

++++++++

once, long, long ago,
i saw you at a club
here in minneapolis,
you and the "arkestra",
all twenty or so of you,
the congas, the saxes,
the young and the old be-bopping

measure after golden measure,
the tall and lovely nubian dancers
melting their way thru the crowd.

and i stood, not ten feet away,
as butterflies emerged
from your endlessness,
your fingertips floating
out over the audience,
flickering here and there
and then wandering to the ceiling,
disappearing into the darkness,
you keyboarding
whole dances and nations of sound
round and round in spinning circles
across this and that galaxy,
this and that star system.

i was very impressed.

+++++++

dear mr. ra,
may your life on saturn
be all and more
than you expected.

and may you return to us,
here on earth,
at your earliest possible
convenience,

as we are bogged down here
in miscellaneous and endless
gray, inhuman insanities.

and you, kind sir,
you always seemed
to have the smell of roses
at your feet.

river town

the morning is young.
everything is clear after last night's rain
here in this little river town,
lost so close to the cities,
lost along the green bluffs.

last night, deep asleep,
a bolt of thunder
split the darkness open.
i jumped out of bed,
wide awake in a split second:

this is the moment

you have waited

your entire life for !

the poplar leaves

today,

the poplar leaves

applaud the very nature of existence.

and whatever it is that i am

applauds

those poplar leaves.

on pondering the state of the democracy

(for robert bly)

what would robert do?

it's not often one has a real mentor,
real teachers in this world are rare.

often you don't understand
what they said

'til they're long gone.

it's raining

it's raining,
gray out.
i listen to doves.

who is it that is doing the listening?
where is this self that everyone wants to empower?
why must i hurry back to the city today?

the reviewer in the blog "hypoallergic"
used words like "invigilator" and "oleaginous"
when he talked about "documenta 14" in athens.

there is a flatness to this kind of discussion.
the art world is a very flat place.

the doves on the telephone line above me
burst into flame.
the rain explodes into pure and clean mathematics.
it is racing sideways down main street,
running exactly and quietly downhill
to the sailboat marina
and this lake where even rough fish have a home.

no one will sail today.
no one will buy a $25 entrée
at the "harbor view café".
the tourists have all gone home, thank god.

i, however, will sit in my chair,
listen to the rain,
and forgive the world all its posturing.

but, who will forgive me?
who will forgive me my posturing?

it's raining,
gray out.

i listen
to doves.

a thousand stars

it's cold as shit out there.
the dog's hiding from me
at the mere mention
of heading outdoors.
she's gotta poop sometime though.
so i layer her in dog sweaters,
silly dog sweaters,
and hide me in layer after layer
of silk and flannel and wool
and down
and i head out.

snow squeaks loud loud loud
as i clomp clomp down dark streets,
making my less than merry rounds,

stars o god so bright, so bright,
heavens so black,
heavens so close,
so close.

suddenly i hear kathy young
and the innocents:

"each night i count the stars in the sky
hoping that you aren't telling me lies"

(o god i'm having a nostalgia relapse)

"you're with me tonight,
i'm captured by your charms,
oh, pretty baby, won't you

hold me in your arms?
a thousand stars in the sky..."

its below zero freezing out
and suddenly i'm back in seventh grade
and jesus i'm chasing jan maxwell
all around saint louis park,
a doggerel adolescent cocktail mix
of true love and not so awakened
quasi-intelligent sentience
girdled by an overdose
of high quality pure
junior high hormones.

then, just as suddenly,
the words of jalāl ad-dīn muhammad balkhī
fall on me:

"we are stars wrapped in skin"

and i see that we are all madly loved,
madly loved, madly loved,
constantly and always held and caressed,
even in the depth of cold,
even in the depth of hardship
even in the depth of darkness.

and even as i race home with the dog,
even as i climb back into my nice warm bed,
even as i run from the furious
knife edge world we live in,
the world of fear and desperate suffering
and the cold, the deep cold,

even then,

i feel the One
who's heart is the beginning
and end of all things,
the beginning and end of all things,
this moment,
this god awful, crushing moment,
this glorious, golden, crushing moment,
this moment of jasmine and lily,
of phlox and dandelion,
this moment of gentle whiteness
blanketing lake and bluffs forever.

dougie sez:

there is a great embrace inside this cold,
there is a wonderful sweetness
inside this cold.
inside this desperate, dark,
nasty-ass winter night
is an invitation to true and lasting joy:

dance on that knife edge tonight!

sing until you are hoarse!

the circus gets serious

1.

the expensive shoes always seem to hurt.
the fog is way too deep to see across the river.
the art absolutely will not make itself.
do i live that far from the capitols of war?

2.

a long and tired night
here in my favorite chair,
a brown leather recliner
lodged in the corner
between my bed and the window.

3.

today the circus gets serious.
today the big top goes up.
the big cats come out of the cages
and start their prowling,
start their growling.
the tiny ballerinas
stand atop the massive horses.
the clowns unroll their smiles.
no more nets underneath the trapeze act,
no more rehearsals to explore.
tonight, everyone pays to attend,
no refunds at the door.

an ambush of poets

the book says it's

a "convocation" of eagles
and a "parliament" of owls,
but a "murder" of crows
and an "unkindness" of ravens.

do i detect a hierarchy about the bird world?
a social system centuries old
that denotes who sits in front of the class,
who gets champagne with dinner,
who gets to wear chanel and who must
wear dickies work jeans?

add to that a "gang" of buffalo or elk,
a "gang" of weasels, or even turkeys.
add to that a "sloth" of bears, a "prickle"
of porcupines, a "skulk" of foxes,
and a "stench" of skunks - and
you can begin to see the problem here.

then, if you leave north america,
you might find yourself with
a "shadow" of jaguars,
a "conspiracy" of lemurs,
a "pandemonium" of parrots,
a "crash" of rhinoceroses,
an "ambush" of tigers.

exactly.
stereotyping.

remember, not all hippies with long hair
were stoners. (well, most were. i plead guilty.)

not all punkers with mohawks were pissed off
loudmouths. (well, again, most were.)

shit, not all businessmen in suits in the
financial district are assholes.
(ok, this one's a no-brainer.)

but really, don't owls care if they are a "parliament"?
and how do the bears feel about being called "slothful"?
and isn't calling a group of skunks a "stink"
pretty much sticking them in a box, a nasty ass
stinky, biased box?

plus, how does a jaguar feel about being forced into
the role of "shadow", i mean doesn't that lead to the
wrong kind of behavior, a youth spent in detention,
an adult life lost behind bars in angola or vacaville?

now, i'm gonna move the adjectives just one
notch down the list, just for fun, just cause
streaming t.v. shows has, yes, become boring
during this pandemic and maybe, just
maybe, this will be more interesting.

thus, we would have:

an "ambush" of toads
a "gang" of turtles
a "cloud" of bears
a "swarm" of buffalo
a "caravan" of cats
a "drove" of eagles

a "skulk" of frogs
a "cackle" of jaguars
a "mob" of lemurs
a "pride" of moles
a "barrel" of mules
a "prickle" of rabbits
an "unkindness" of rhinoceroses
a "fever" of swans
a "pandemonium" of pigs

i mean, isn't that just a whole lot better?

now let's try to see what we can do
if i toy with our human species:

a "skulk" of republicans
a "cackle" of rock stars
a "barrel" of movie stars
a "mob" of girl scouts
a "pride" of ministers
a "conspiracy" of artists
a "cackle" of priests
a "swarm" of media consultants
a "prickle" of police
a "murder" of musicians
a "pandemonium" of progressives

and, yes,

an "ambush" of poets.

on kurt vonnegut's assignment to school kids and their teachers: 6 lines

time to sit still this spring morning, sit still here in the big city.

later, my dog and i will drive the hour and a half south along the mighty mississippi

to my lovely studio in a lovely, little wisconsin river town

where i will create art ceaselessly and recklessly and, yes, even carefully,

thinking all the while of the time we brought kurt vonnegut to my college

to dynamite the brains of youngsters that that thought they knew it all.

standoff

harassed by a loud-mouthed
gray squirrel
six feet over my head
up in the branches of the maple,
my coonhound stella and i
ponder what to do.

then, getting up,
moving around the table,
i look the critter in the eye
and tell him to fuck off.

he stares back at me,
lifts his tail, arches his back
and makes a long irritating,
clicking noise.

we've got a standoff,
it appears.

similes

i'm thinking about using similes in my poetry.

i don't usually partake in them,
they seem so darn obvious.
but perhaps i should try again,
they're all the rage in the poetry world.

yes, i'm going to use similes like mad.

wait, i'm not sure that's a good start.

i will write like a bull
chasing naked lutherans
thru abandoned art museums
on the 4th of july
in jutland, in denmark,
just there on the beach
where the north sea
becomes the baltic.

no, i don't think that's exactly it either.

perhaps, i should research this.
maybe this will help:

"now a simile, as the name imports,
is a comparison of two or more things,
more or less unlike in themselves,
for the purpose of illustration."

exactly.

thus, Wordsworth:

"Thy soul was like a Star, and dwelt apart;
Thou hadst a voice whose sound was like the sea"

wow. wonderful. perfect.

my turn:

dougie's dream world mind,
like fireflies on a summer's night,
blinks on and off, on and off,
wanders here and there,

wanders here and there.

3 koans

the eagles along the valley walls are not afraid
to roost where they can be easily seen.

the coyotes following the railroad tracks are not
disturbed by the skyscrapers nearby.

a falcon nesting high atop the riverside condos
preys on the sparrows my wife feeds every day.

i am living inside louise erdrich's novels now

i am living inside louise erdrich's novels now,
The Antelope Wife, A Plague of Doves,
The Last Report on The Miracles at Little No Horse,
Tales of Burning Love.

i can't stop, all fourteen in a year and a half:
sweetheart calico's ragged, dark teeth,
the desperate sweat stink of jack mauser,
the long, elastic jokes of nanapush,
the wooden sighs of elaine in the nunnery
late at night.

when I run out of louise,
it's the falling down drunk hopeless
william h. macy in "shameless" on netflix,
his grimace smile-face all whiskered
and wrinkled and torn.

or the antics of russel peters on youtube,
insulting everyone in his audience,
the audience responding with endless glee,
wiping tears of joy from their eyes
as he lambasts their race, their sex,
their intelligence.

then, i mix in more books:
The Rise of Fascism by f. l. carsten,
Psychic Tarot by nancy antenucci,
Revolutionary Letters by diane di prima,
and anything by jim harrison.
then, i add a magazine article on vultures,

another on wisconsin wolves, and
way too many facebook essays on trump
and trumpism.

add to that my coonhound's entirely
too incessant howling at squirrels
on the deck, facetime talks with
grandkids in mazatlan and san diego,
and walks on the ice covered jetty,
23 degrees below one day,
36 above the next.

what makes us humans demand so much input,
endless story after story after story?
why do we decorate everything we touch,
decorate it with every color and form
and imagining under the sun?
and why do we insist that form
not be emptiness?

haven't we read and discussed
the "heart sutra"?

or did we sleep thru that class?

the mysteries

dictionary.com says that a mystery
is "any truth that is unknowable
except by divine revelation".

when i google "the mysteries"
i get 115 million hits.

wiki says
that "mysteries were religious schools
of the greco-roman world
for which participation
was reserved to initiates."

schools to teach the unknowable?
schools to create divine revelation?

i think i'll start one.
my mystery school will be called:
"blue moon mystery school"

- catchy, eh?

(a blue moon is the second full moon
in one calendar month,
it is somewhat rare
only happening every two to three years.
it's also a brewing company based
out of golden, colorado.)

actually, i'm more interested
in the number one hit "blue moon"
by the marcels.

it was a big smash on the charts in 1961
and had that great bass voice line:
"blue, blue, blue, blue moon,
dip sha dip, sha dip,
blue, blue, blue, blue moon"...
i was thirteen and hormones
were kicking holes in my brain
while livestock roamed my tight jeans.
back then we all watched the dick clark show
after school at sue stafne's house
cause both her parents worked
and i was always trying to get lucky,
which of course i didn't,
though not from lack of trying.

but god didn't cheri johnson
look hot in her capri pants
at lunch time out in the hall
where we gathered
after we ate as quick as possible
and danced slow
with the dream girl
of our choice
in front of
almost
everyone?

i gotta get back on the horse

(for ted king)

i gotta get back on the horse.
the poems are alluding me.
i saw a couple duck in a doorway
back there a few blocks,
over by the post office.

yesterday i thought i saw one
in the "third base bar",
in the corner
near the bathrooms.
(i swear i don't really go in there,
at least not much).

and i heard that a couple of poems
might be hanging out down in nelson
at that cheezy hotel they have there,
the one off of 35 on the road to wabasha,
across from the fireworks stand.

how do i lure them back
to this neck of the woods,
to my studio
where i can rework them
into oblivion?

i'm thinking of just leaving
a thesaurus by the front door.
i don't think they can resist that.

and next to it i'll put that photo

of ginsberg with kerouac back in the day.
that should do the trick,
they always go for "the beats".

brutal #1

i want to write about the cold.

it was brutal cold today. again.
around 12 below,
minus 20 with the wind.

it was so cold
the snow squeaked beneath my boots.
so cold
i wore crampons
to navigate the glare ice
i could not quite see
beneath the snow.

now i hurry through my dog walk,
down village streets,
dim and dumb,
watching stella sniff the air,
sniff the yellow snow,
oblivious to the edge of pain
that surrounds us,
happy,
dog happy.

i grind through my time outdoors,
not looking up at the trees
shadowed against the dark sky,
not looking at the moon shouting
against the silvery night,
mercury low on the evening horizon,
as loud as i've ever seen it.

i have no room for enjoyment tonight,
i just wanna get this job done.
praise god stella will poop,
and i can bag it,
find a trash can nearby
and race back to the warmth.
warmth is heaven.

brutal #2

we live in a sea of cold here
in wisconsin, in minnesota.
sea birds of ice descend in winter,
rape and pillage our flesh,
annihilate our prayers,
scavenge our desperation,
long to crush and devour
each and every last carcass of joy
we can muster.

most folks here
hole up for days on end,
anxious to avoid their bodies,
they seem to forget completely
how to leave the house.

but me, i've left the city.

where i live now,
rabbits grow lightly
below the lower branches
of elder and birch
out near the frozen-up
chippewa river
bottoms.

where i live now,
turkeys sprint across
the snow-driven fields,
wild in their lust
for an easier life
somewhere south of here

near alma.

where i live now,
owls wait for that first move
the mouse takes tonight,
that first dash
across the hardened snow crust
to the easy joys
of the granary bin.

fields of the lord

the cursor jumped around the page
last night as i wrote on my computer.
it has a mind of its own sometimes.
my heart jumps around in my chest as i sleep.
it also seems to have a mind of its own.

now, the room is very dark.
the beginnings of morning
touch the edges of the window curtains.
i have been tired before from bad sleep,
it happens.
i will be tired again.

and now i have slipped
into the spirit world.
there are too many ghost beings
gliding past my seeing-ness.
there are faces wherever i look,
they are watching me.
i am learning to watch them.
when i lean into their world,
it seems crowded.
when they edge into mine,
they seem ill at ease
with my presence.

but what is my job here?

or am i simply playing
in the fields of the lord?

wild thing

standing on the jetty above the freezing lake,
i watch the bright stars in the dark night

and wonder how 30 years have passed

since that moment
when we danced down the aisle

to sister carol chanting:

"wild thing,

you make my heart sing,

you make everything,

groovy..."

the light is too flat

1.

i don't like the middle of the day much.
the light is too flat,
the smells are too strong,
too pungent,
too vigorous.
it is very hard to see angels during the day,
the spirit world in general, actually.
it is too easy to spot concrete sidewalks,
gas stations sprinting for the suburbs,
high school equations on chalk boards,
parking spots reserved
for small town bank presidents.

no, dusk and dawn are always best,
though a dark night is good too.
and midnight with a hazy big moon
across the water
is double holy,
of course.

2.

i think i'd like to hole up like a bear.
find a spot in the side of a hill,
a kind of a cave,
not very deep,
dry and shady,
with a nice view of the valley.

there i would ponder bodhidarma
and magritte and bach, coltrane,
the finns as a people in general,
and how long it takes to really
cook a pot roast
(not that i can cook).

the cave would be a nice one,
smallish, down river
along the mississippi on the wisconsin side
so i could catch the setting sun
pulling oranges and pinks
and maybe golds
out of gangly, skinny clouds,
clouds heading west,
heading for the cities
and a chance to make it big
in media or politics
or misplaced casino monies.

no, i'd stay right here in my cave
'til the light begins to dim,
at which point i would have a much better chance
to skip between layers,
and drop this fleshy animal skin
for the good of all things
both lovely and small,

drop this skin like a house robe
to the kitchen floor,
drop it and wander into to the fog worlds,
creek songs you can taste
on the inside edges of your tongue.

then, once firmly ensconced

near the rim of the cave,
placed exactly at the edge,
i would address bear time,
that world of slow winters,
that ghost of thickness
as a kind of light,
right there,
hidden from cold and sound.
right there,
where bear sleep rises
into

moon

light.

taking a bath

taking a bath, reading *Dharma Bums*
for about the 4th time,
i suddenly miss katagiri roshi
and the old days:

"emptiness is form, form is emptiness."

don't get caught on either side of that one!

sit down hard in both at once,
each moment immaculate and true.

nothing is better than a good hot bath!

walk away

(for hannah and eli)

walk away

and wander the glorious garden
that blake lived in.

remember
that there are angels

in all things,
at all times,

no matter how weak your eyesight has grown,

no matter how callous your heart.

the days and nights have become fluid

the days and nights have become fluid,
a kind of water.

but not the kind of water
you buy in stores.
not the kind of water that pours from springs
or erupts from wells.
not the water that hangs along the bottom
of your glass,
suspended in fluoride.

no, a kind of water more like fire.
like tequila or mescal
(and i don't mean the good stuff).
water more like the morning sun
on the horizon
when it's hot enough
that you can feel the sunshine burn into your skin
even when it's 7 a.m.,
even when the light is distant
and untouchable.

like say in india.

the cows are still moving slowly thru the streets.
they have been moving thru the streets all night.
they don't really have homes,
no one feeds them.
they are skinny,
the down side of being sacred.
the sadhus are skinny too.
i smoke ganja with them in a hovel

alongside the flooded river
next to the burning ghats,
the poor buried nearby,
their bones washing to the surface
in the monsoon rains.

"om siva shankara hari hari ganja!"
the sadhu shouts
and takes an enormous toke on his clay chillum,
the smoke eventually finding its way
to the heaven in his eyes.

how did i survive those days?
how will i survive these?

and where is my guru now that i need him?
i've searched the astral for years -
all i get is a dream once in a while,
a honkin' dream.
its nepal, not india,
i've never been to nepal.
i'm alone, or susan is with me,
or i am traveling with another sannyasin,
another devotee.
we wander the marketplace, always the market.
we can't find our way.
but i'm not anxious,
i can feel him,
i can feel the way the moon shoots off his body
towards me, towards the flowers
behind me, the flowers
beside the road.
they are lilies, he is always
surrounded by lilies.

so was my father at the funeral.
death is a kind of water.
and i just think death might be fluid.

lilies are not fluid tho,
they are white,
bright white.
they have a smell
that releases one from the body
and allows the angels
to sing slowly
and carry one,
whatever one might actually be,
to the other side,
the slower side,
the side that is not made of meat
and gravel
and the morning news.

some days are hard
and i long to touch the other side,
to see my grandfather again,
my great-grandfather.
but i have grandchildren myself now,
a wife i adore,
a dog to walk along this gorgeous lake.
i need to stay.

besides, the paintings are pouring out,
the poems have no end.
the leaves must return to the trees.
the water must return to the ground.

"guinea pig social hour"

(for schnauzer)

"guinea pig social hour"
11 a.m. to 1 p.m. today,
chuck and don's pet food outlet,
8711 east point douglas road,
cottage grove.

"hoppy hour",
a social hour for rabbits and their owners,
1-2 p.m. sunday, $3,
animal humane society,
845 north meadow lane,
golden valley.

ok, somebody at the paper
has gotta be making this stuff up.
they're bored with writing obituaries.
the twins are off today,
the vikings have left training camp.
everybody is tired of whatever nonsense
trump is spouting at his enemies,
which is pretty much the entire world.

no, this staff writer needs to do
what every other good employee
would be doing on the clock
when no one's watching:
he needs to be writing his rom-com screenplay,
starring ryan gosling and jennifer lawrence,
staged in the colorado rockies at xmas.
writing the one where jen's

mother is sick with cancer,
but makes a miraculous recovery
after gosling comes back
from running off to new york city
with mila kunis,
his tail between his legs now,
a humble hunk
finally.

eddie

eddie's in st. cloud prison.
i am at silver lake park.

he is sitting in a 10 foot by 8 foot room
with concrete walls.
most likely he is lying on his bed
staring at the ceiling.

i am sitting on a patio looking out over the lake.
birds are singing here.
there is shade and sunny skies.
folks wander by talking about this or that.
some are doing landscape paintings.

eddie gets out of his cell two hours a day.
he's supposed to get transferred at some point,
god knows where.

i wander around most days,
over to the river to walk the dog,
around the back yard following my lawnmower,
off to the coffee shop to sit and write.
some days i drive an hour and a half
to pepin and my studio there,
alongside the mighty mississippi.

they can't seem to get eddie
reading glasses that work,
so he doesn't read much.
he also doesn't get all his meds.
that can't be good.

some days at the studio i paint for hours,
taking the occasional break to visit
the little grocery store down the block
or grab a hamburger at the bar
around the corner.
sometimes i sit and look at art books,
laying in my hammock in the back yard.

eddie said he doesn't want duane and i
to visit, says he's too weepy,
says he couldn't handle seeing us.
i'm not even sure that cindy
is allowed to visit him.
(i hear that they talk on the phone
for five minutes a day).

i will have to send eddie my poems,
my dreams, my drawings…
i'm not sure what else to do.
maybe once he's got the right glasses
i'll send him aurobindo's book,
the one where he talks
about being a revolutionary
and waking up to the cosmic laws
of the universe
during his long years in prison.

or maybe i'll just paint him a picture
of this great lake,
23 miles long, 3 miles across,
steel blue under a baby blue sky,
bluffs and coulees across the river
all kinds of green,
everything as gorgeous
as the scotland i see in my books.

++++++++++

may the gods and goddesses that created
the beauty outside my window
find eddie where he sits today
and lighten his load.

may they dance lightly with his soul
in the middle of the sleeping night,
in the middle of his darkest thoughts,
in the middle of his sinking down
into the prison floor.

may all who read this poem
find love in their hearts
and may he feel that wonderful love
sitting in his cell,
buried behind walls of fear and anger
and distrust.

and may all beings know awakening.

i am studying blake again

(a diatribe)

i am studying william blake again.
he talked about angels a lot.
i talk about angels more and more
as i get older and older.
and older.

i talk about how the sides of their heads
so uniquely match their wings,
about how their wings are half
the size of the space
between their teeth,
about how their teeth
are sheathed in a kind of gold
only found in new guinea
under trees the size of small
ant hills.

yet blake is an unpopular subject
with the art world crowd.
more likely "semiotics",
"de-colonialism",
or "post-structuralism"
swim from the sides of their silted mouths,
mouths embedded in enameled statuary
lodged in the darkened corners
of empty urban mausoleums
where gehard richter,
jeff koons,
and marina abramovic
have gathered to mortgage our futures,

where they and their ilk
re-process the sounds of fog,
rework and regurgitate the ecstatic moment
most often known as sunrise,
re-infect and disembody, re-birth
the lifeless, the vapid...

+++++++++

just now morning drips ever so slowly
from black ash trees
in the quiet sloughs
down below czechville,
just south of where 88 hits 35,
down near the whitman bottoms,
down in duck hunting country,
down in the land that art forgot.

this chance

Appearances are mind and emptiness is mind.
Thoughts are mind and delusion is mind.
Origination is mind and cessation is mind.
May we cut through all conceptual embellishments
in the mind.
                     - Karmapa Rangjung Dorjé

this chance to differentiate myself
between light and matter
astounds me.

i am light, i am light,
i am a hunk of flesh.

there is no me,
there is no not me.

where do i end and xavier begins?
and ted, what about ted?
why is susan as much inside me as outside me?
my grandchildren are alive inside my heart.
my children are me, are not me, are me...

and this river, isn't this river me,
wave after wave after wave?
and the squirrels playing on the maples,
what about them?
do i get to pick and choose?

o, god in the heavens

or whoever or whatever
is in charge here,

elucidate if you will...

please.

twelve twelve seventeen

(for s.j.)

i have been trying to write you a love poem for years
(easier to bang my head against a wall)

but there is no way my words can fly
farther than this:

touching the exact perfect scent
of the back of your neck,

i find my way home

after so many lifetimes

lost at sea.

toboggan

my god, i slept 8 hours last night.
nine, if you count the time i dozed in my chair,
the laptop on my lap,
a cheezy mexican netflix show
blaring away
as i faded in and out.

praise god for the little pill i took last night.
i do it every once in awhile
when i get tired
of trying to sleep thru the pain,
a scrawny grey mole
rooted down deep along my spine,
gnawing his way to the surface,
leaving shreds of bone and cartilage
on the floor beside the bed.

yes, i write this song
in praise of pharmaceuticals,
tho all my young friends
who claim i can right this floundering ship
with kale chips
and gluten free pancakes
would be aghast
and agog.

meditating daily
for most of 49 years,
swimming as best i can,
walking,
and old fart yoga
not enough to match the plundering of time,

not enough for all the football and soccer,
the construction crews,
the years of wild hippie dancing.

i'm sure the canadian geese
i heard honking across the black night sky
as i walked last night after dinner
don't touch pills
though they launch themselves forward
for a thousand miles every fall,
battling anxious winds and weathers,
'til sunny skies
and heartbreakingly sweet grasses
bring them back to earth,
bone tired at the end
of their journey.

no, today i'll parade around my studio
in some kind of mind dream
lost weekend palette of making,
the occasional orgasm of delight
here and there
when a drawing finishes itself,
when a painting is being birthed,

when the angels first enter the room
and take their stools besides me,
close enough so that i don't get lost
from their world completely,
far away enough
that they can nap when they need to
and play cards without me
looking over their shoulders
and commenting on misplays
and lost moves.

dougie sez:

may all who trudge uphill in this life
find themselves at the top
with a good strong toboggan
and a clear path to the bottom,
the snow just perfect
for a long ride
and a life full of

simple

cheap

thrills.

dougie padilla

long ago and far away i was a young poet. i wrote constantly. then came the viet nam war and all the protests. and then came san francisco and psychedelics and communes around the country. a psychotic break came. heart failure came. and ashrams and organic farming with horses. eventually, there were kids and houses and marriage and businesses. and even grand-kids...

now it's fifty years later and out of the blue poetry returned quick and sure. i'd moved my art studio to rural wisconsin to beat rising rents in the city, to concentrate on my painting, to meditate, be in nature, to face my aloneness. once there, i started working on my memoirs. instead, poems begin pouring out. now five years later they continue to pour out. what a blessing.

2020, pepin, wisconsin

www.dougiepadillapoet.com

www.ingramcontent.com/pod-product-compliance
Lightning Source LLC
Chambersburg PA
CBHW031203090426
42736CB00009B/773